WORLD EXPLORERS

JOHN CABOT

Kristin Petrie

Checkerboard
Library

An Imprint of Abdo Publishing
abdobooks.com

ABDOBOOKS.COM

Published by Abdo Publishing, a division of ABDO, PO Box 398166, Minneapolis, Minnesota 55439. Copyright © 2022 by Abdo Consulting Group, Inc. International copyrights reserved in all countries. No part of this book may be reproduced in any form without written permission from the publisher. Checkerboard Library™ is a trademark and logo of Abdo Publishing.

Printed in the United States of America, North Mankato, Minnesota
102021
012022

Design and Production: Tamara JM Peterson, Mighty Media, Inc.
Editor: Liz Salzmann
Cover Photograph: Photo Researchers/Alamy Photo
Interior Photographs: Bettmann/Getty Images, p. 15; Birdiegal/Shutterstock Images, pp. 27, 29 (bottom); Denis Burdin/Shutterstock Images, pp. 16–17; Giustino Menescardi/Wikimedia Commons, pp. 4, 28 (top); g215/Shutterstock Images, pp. 7, 28 (bottom); Hans Dahl/Wikimedia Commons, pp. 5, 28 (top); Library of Congress, pp. 23, 29 (top); Michael Sittow/Wikimedia Commons, p. 13; MicroOne/Shutterstock Images, pp. 20–21; Nigel Jarvis/Shutterstock Images, p. 19; North Wind Picture Archives/Alamy Photo, pp. 9, 10–11; Pictures From History/Alamy Photo, p. 12; THEPALMER/iStockphoto, pp. 24–25
Design Elements: Joseph Moxon/Flickr (map), Oleg Iatsun/Shutterstock Images (compass rose)

Library of Congress Control Number: 2021942982

Publisher's Cataloging-in-Publication Data
Names: Petrie, Kristin, author.
Title: John Cabot / by Kristin Petrie
Description: Minneapolis, Minnesota : Abdo Publishing, 2022 | Series: World explorers | Includes online resources and index.
Identifiers: ISBN 9781532197253 (lib. bdg.) | ISBN 9781098219383 (ebook)
Subjects: LCSH: Cabot, John, -1498?--Juvenile literature. | Discovery and exploration--Juvenile literature. | Exploring expeditions--Juvenile literature. | Explorers--Biography--Juvenile literature.
Classification: DDC 970.01--dc23

CONTENTS

JOHN CABOT 4
JOHN'S CHILDHOOD 6
BEFORE EXPLORING 8
A SHORTER ROUTE 10
PLANNING 12
FAILED ATTEMPT 16
LAND HO! 18
THE GREAT ADMIRAL 22
FINAL VOYAGE 26
TIMELINE 28
GLOSSARY 30
SAYING IT 31
ONLINE RESOURCES 31
INDEX 32

JOHN CABOT

Explorers from Scandinavia were some of the first people to sail across the North Atlantic Ocean. By the 1000s, Scandinavians had already settled on Iceland and Greenland.

Around the year 1000, Scandinavian Leif Eriksson and his crew were sailing in the North Atlantic. They landed on a new coast, which they called Vinland. Many scientists now believe they were the first Europeans on the island of Newfoundland, Canada.

No one else from Europe traveled across the North Atlantic during the next 500 years. Then Italian explorer John Cabot made his first voyage to North America. He bravely sailed into **uncharted** seas not knowing what he would find.

John Cabot

Leif Eriksson (*left*)

JOHN'S CHILDHOOD

Giovanni Caboto was born in Genoa, Italy, in 1450. Today, we know him as John Cabot. Little is known about John's childhood. But we do know that his family moved to Venice, Italy, in 1461.

John's father, Guilio, was a seaman and merchant. He owned a spice shop in Venice. At that time, spices came mostly from Asia. They were very valuable.

John helped his father at the shop. Guilio may have talked about the faraway lands where the spices came from. That could have been when John began to dream about exploring the world.

WOULD YOU?
Would you rather be a merchant like Guilio, or an explorer like John? Why would you choose that career?

Venice has many waterways that are used like streets. To this day, people get around Venice in boats.

BEFORE EXPLORING

John's formal education is not known. However, the Cabotos were fortunate to have lived in wealthy cities with good schools. So, John and other children from Genoa and Venice were able to attend classes. They studied subjects such as reading, writing, and art.

John also became interested in sailing. From an early age, he studied mapmaking. He read the book *The Travels of Marco Polo*. And he dreamed of sailing the open seas.

As an adult, John followed in his father's footsteps and became a spice merchant. He sailed the Mediterranean Sea between Italy and Egypt. On these trips, he traded Italian goods for Eastern spices.

In about 1482, Cabot married a woman named Mattea. They had three sons, named Lewis, Sebastian, and Sanctus. The family lived in Italy and Spain before moving to Bristol, England, in the 1490s.

Cabot also spent time in London, England.

A SHORTER ROUTE

Shortly before Cabot settled in England, explorer Christopher Columbus made a discovery. In 1492, he sailed west from Spain, crossed the Atlantic Ocean, and reached land. Everyone believed this land was an area of Asia known as the Indies, or Spice Islands.

Cabot also wanted to sail to Asia. But he believed there was a shorter route than the one Columbus took. Cabot's mapmaking knowledge had taught him something important. Because the world is round, the farther north you are on a map, the closer the **longitudes** are to each other.

Cabot figured it would be possible to get to Asia much faster by starting farther north. He decided to sail from England. This plan would have worked, except for one thing. Cabot didn't know that North America was in his way.

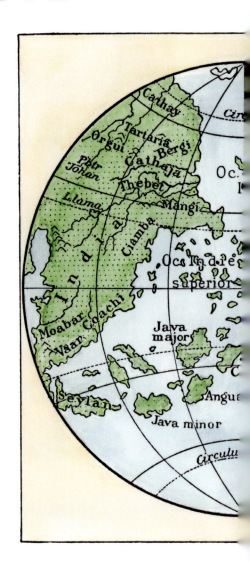

In 1492, Europeans did not know North and South America existed. This map shows their knowledge of the world.

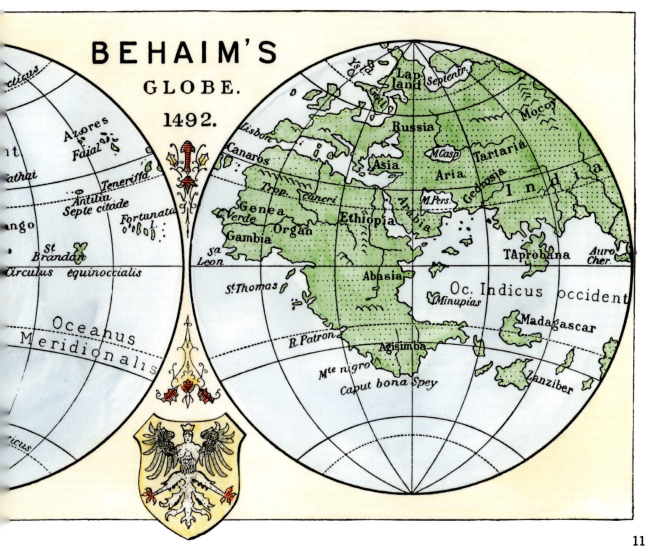

PLANNING

Living in Bristol, England, helped Cabot develop his plan. One reason for this was that Bristol was one of the largest and most important seaports in England. Several expeditions had recently left from there.

Another reason was that the English government was willing to fund the trip. Cabot had been having trouble getting money to pay for his voyage. Most countries were sending their explorers east to find trading routes to Asia. Cabot wanted to go west.

Unfortunately, it was hard to convince people to give him money to test his plan. Both King John II of Portugal and King Ferdinand of Spain refused Cabot's request for money. But Cabot's luck changed in 1496.

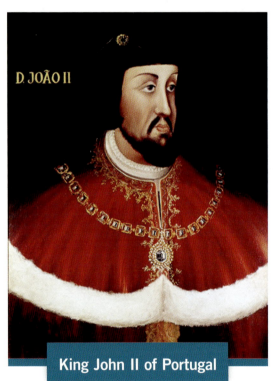

King John II of Portugal

King Ferdinand of Spain

King Henry VII of England agreed to help Cabot finance his voyage. Businesses in Bristol also agreed to help Cabot. They hoped to profit from his discoveries.

WOULD YOU?
Would you give money to a dreamer like John Cabot? Why or why not?

Europeans believed that China and Japan were rich in gold, **gems**, spices, and silks. Henry VII hoped John Cabot would find a faster route to these riches. This would make England the greatest trading center in the world.

In addition, Henry VII knew that he could become rich if Cabot's theories were right. Cabot was to give the king one-fifth of any profit he made on his journey. In March 1496, Henry VII gave Cabot permission to sail as a representative of England.

The king wrote a **patent** for the expedition. He wrote that Cabot should seek and discover "whatsoever islands, countries, regions or **provinces** . . . which before this time were unknown to all Christians."

Cabot presenting his plan to King Henry VII in 1496

FAILED ATTEMPT

In 1496, Cabot set sail from Bristol, England, with one ship. His mission was to find a **Northwest Passage** to Asia. Cabot was the first European explorer to attempt this voyage.

Cabot may have been the first because sailing so far north was dangerous. The ocean water was often icy. The wooden ships of that time could not hold up to the ice. Also, the North Atlantic was unexplored. So, he and his crew didn't know what they'd face there. This, too, was scary.

Unfortunately, after reaching nearby Iceland, Cabot had to return to England. A food **shortage** and arguments with his crew forced him to turn back. Dangerous waters and fear of the unknown also helped end this first attempt.

WOULD YOU?

Would you brave the **uncharted**, icy waters of the North? Why do you think John Cabot turned back on his first voyage?

Giant icebergs hindered explorers' attempts to find the Northwest Passage.

LAND HO!

On May 20, 1497, Cabot sailed out of the Bristol seaport again. He had a crew of just 18 sailors. Their ship was named the *Matthew*.

The *Matthew* was small for this type of voyage. It was about 78 feet (23.7 m) long and 20.5 feet (6.3 m) wide. The *Matthew* could carry about 50 tons (45 t) of cargo.

Cabot's first stop may have been in Dursey Head, Ireland. From there, the crew set out for Asia. At least, that's what they thought they were doing. On June 24, 1497, they sighted land. Cabot believed they had reached Asia. The crew went ashore, and Cabot claimed the land for England.

Exactly where Cabot and his crew landed is unknown. **Historians** guess that it was any of the areas now known as Nova Scotia, Labrador, Cape Breton Island, or Newfoundland. Still others believe he landed farther south, in what is now Maine. But many believe he landed at Cape Bonavista, Newfoundland.

This replica of the *Matthew* was completed in 1996. In 1997, it sailed to Newfoundland on the anniversary of Cabot's voyage.

19

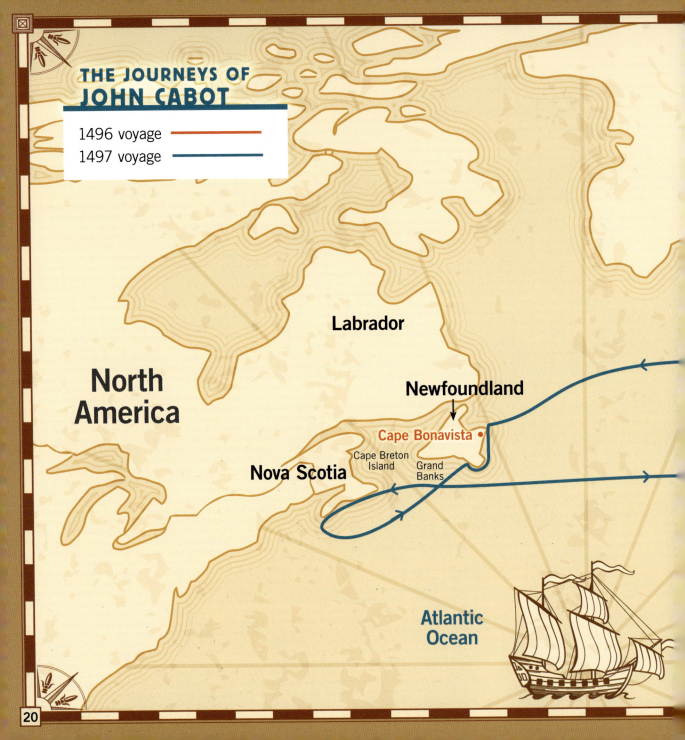

THE GREAT ADMIRAL

Like Christopher Columbus, Cabot thought he had reached Asia. Cabot decided to survey the coastline. He may have explored all the way down to Maine. Some people believe Cabot named many of the east coast's islands and capes.

Cabot did not find the jewels, spices, and other riches he was searching for. However, he did find an **incredible** fishing area. Thousands of cod could be caught just by lowering nets or weighted baskets into the waters. This area of Newfoundland is now called Grand Banks.

After about a month of exploring, the crew headed home. On the return voyage, they took a more southerly route. They landed on the northern coast of France, rather than in England. Finally in August 1497, the *Matthew* and its crew made it back to Bristol, England.

Cabot lands at Cape Bonavista, Newfoundland.

Even though he hadn't found any established cities, Cabot announced that he had reached Asia. So, people thought he had discovered an island off the coast of China.

Cabot was named "The Great Admiral," and King Henry VII rewarded him with the sum of ten English pounds. Today, this would equal about $9,000. Cabot was also given a **pension** of 20 pounds per year for his discovery. This is about $18,000 per year today.

WOULD YOU?

Would you have believed John Cabot when he said he reached Asia? What evidence would you have asked for to **confirm** his story?

Drawings of Cabot often show him meeting Native Americans when he lands on Newfoundland. However, historians don't think he saw any people when he went ashore.

FINAL VOYAGE

The king and merchants of England were pleased with Cabot's success. He received a **patent** for another voyage. In 1498, Cabot left Bristol again. He had five ships, 200 crewmen, and enough supplies to last one year. This time, he planned to sail west or south. The goal was to reach Japan.

Storms and the rough sea forced one of Cabot's ships back to a port in England or Ireland. Unfortunately, no one knows what happened to the other ships, or to Cabot. Some people think Cabot made it to North America. Others believe he was lost at sea. Yet others believe he returned to England after his voyage and died there in 1499.

John Cabot may never have found what he was looking for. However, his explorations opened the way for England's **colonization** of North America. In time, the world would learn the importance of the **landmasses** that were in the way.

There is a statue of Cabot at Cape Bonavista.

TIMELINE

1450
Giovanni Caboto is born in Genoa, Italy. He later becomes known as John Cabot.

1482
Cabot marries Mattea.

1490s
The Cabots settle in Bristol, England.

1461
John's family moves to Venice, Italy.

28

1497

Cabot sails on his second voyage and lands on Newfoundland, Canada. He explores the area and then returns to England.

1496

Cabot starts his first voyage to find a Northwest Passage to Asia. He has to turn back after reaching Iceland.

1498

Cabot sets out on his third voyage with five ships and 200 crewmen. No one is sure what happens to Cabot on this voyage. He may have been lost at sea.

GLOSSARY

colonization—the act of establishing a colony.

confirm—to definitively state or prove true something that was previously uncertain.

gem—a valuable stone cut and polished for decoration, such as jewelry.

historian—a person who studies or writes about history.

incredible—amazing or unbelievable.

landmass—a very large area of land, such as a continent.

longitude—a measure of distance east or west on Earth's surface. On a map, this distance is marked by lines that run from the North Pole to the South Pole.

Northwest Passage—a supposed sea passage along the north coast of North America. It would connect the Pacific and Atlantic oceans.

patent—an official document giving a person the right or privilege to perform an act or duty.

pension—a form of income that workers receive after they retire.

province—a political division of a country.

shortage—when there is not enough of something that is needed.

uncharted—unknown and therefore not recorded on a map, chart, or plan.

SAYING IT

Cape Breton Island—KAYP BREHT-uhn EYE-luhnd

Giovanni Caboto—joh-VAHN-nee kah-BOH-toh

Labrador—LA-bruh-dawr

Mediterranean Sea—meh-duh-tuh-RAY-nee-uhn SEE

Nova Scotia—NOH-vuh SKO-shuh

ONLINE RESOURCES

To learn more about John Cabot, please visit **abdobooklinks.com** or scan this QR code. These links are routinely monitored and updated to provide the most current information available.

INDEX

Asia, 6, 8, 10, 12, 14, 16, 18, 22, 24, 26
Atlantic Ocean, 4, 10, 16

birth, 6

Canada, 4, 18, 22
childhood, 6, 8
China, 14, 24
Columbus, Christopher, 10, 22

death, 26
disappearance, 26

education, 8
Egypt, 8
England, 8, 10, 12, 14, 16, 18, 22, 24, 26
Eriksson, Leif, 4
Europe, 4, 14, 16

family, 6, 8
Ferdinand (king of Spain), 12
France, 22

Greenland, 4

Henry VII (king of England), 14, 24, 26

Iceland, 4, 16
Indies, 10
Ireland, 18, 26
Italy, 6, 8

Japan, 14, 26
John II (king of Portugal), 12

Maine, 18, 22
Matthew, 18, 22
Mediterranean Sea, 8

North America, 4, 10, 26
Northwest Passage, 16

riches, 14, 22

Scandinavia, 4
Spain, 8, 10, 12
Spice Islands, 10
spices, 6, 8, 10, 14, 22

trading, 8, 12, 14
Travels of Marco Polo, The, 8